4TH Grade

Teacher Resource

by Carole Marsh

Editorial Assistant: Chad Beard ● Graphic Designer: Lynette Rowe

ISBN
• 0-635-02520-5 •

**NEW LOOK!
NEW STANDARDS!**
*Test scores have increased
as much as 400%!*

Table of Contents

Carole Marsh Ohio Titles

Ohio Experience Specific Readers—Famous People in the MODEL

Anthony, Susan
..............................RE004

Armstrong, Neil
..............................RE096

Carson, Rachel
..............................RE152

Carver, George Washington
..............................RE018

Drew, Charles
..............................RE156

Edison, Thomas
..............................RE093

Jefferson, Thomas
..............................RE007

Kettering, Charles
..............................RE153

King Jr., Martin Luther
..............................RE008

Lincoln, Abraham
..............................RE005

Morgan, Garrett
..............................RE154

Tecumseh
..............................RE094

Truth, Sojourner
..............................RE120

Tubman, Harriet
..............................RE011

Washington, George
..............................RE001

Woods, Granville
..............................RE155

Wright Brothers
..............................RE091

The Ohio Experience™ Curriculum Series:

Kindergarten	First Grade	Second Grade
Third Grade	Fourth Grade	Fifth Grade

Ohio Experience Reference Guide

20 Ways to Teach the MODEL with Pizzazz!

The Ohio Experience Book

Fourth Grade Curriculum:

4th Grade Student Workbook

4th Grade Student Workbook, Teacher's Edition

4th Grade Teacher's Resource Guide

4th Grade Test Prep CD

Ohio State Stuff:

Ohio Experience Poster/Map

Ohio Experience Biographies Book

Ohio Facts & Factivities! CD-ROM

Let's Discover Ohio! CD-ROM

The BIG Ohio Reproducible Activity Book

My First Book About Ohio!

Ohio Jeopardy!: Answers and Questions About Our State

Ohio "Jography!": A Fun Run Through Our State

My First Pocket Guide: Ohio

The Ohio Coloring Book

Ohio Stickers

Ohio Biography Bingo Game

Ohio Geography Bingo Game

Ohio History Bingo Game

Ohio State Stuff Bookmarks

Ohio Millionaire GameBook

Ohio Wheel of Fortune GameBook

Ohio Survivor GameBook

Ohio BIG State Wall Timeline

Ohio State Student Reference Timeline

Other Series:

African American Heritage Series

Native American Heritage Series

Hispanic Heritage Series

Other Related Books:

Orville & Wilbur Wright Step Out Into The Sky!

Dear Educator,

Well, here you are—with the enormous challenge of teaching your students all you can from the Academic Content Standards. After spending months deeply involved in the Ohio Experience, I know just how you feel—there is so much information and not enough time to cover it all! I was asking myself, "Did I really cover all the standards?" Rest assured, all of the standards are covered in the Ohio Experience student workbook.

The Ohio Experience covers all the social studies standards including history, people in societies, geography, economics, government, and citizenship. This course is designed to help prepare students to understand people and places throughout the rest of their lives. As an employer of young people over the years, I see what a wonderful advantage a person new to the work world enjoys when he or she can communicate even a basic understanding of how the world works right where he or she lives and works.

Social studies is a fascinating course of study. It's easy to see how influences from many societies have created a rich "melting pot" of culture. You'll also see how important it is that people work together for their common good. The Ohio Experience will open students' eyes to the world around them.

I have learned a lot by researching and writing The Ohio Experience books and other products. So come along with me and enjoy your very own Ohio Experience—it's the trip of a lifetime!

Carole Marsh

As European cultures spread west across the Alleghenies into the Ohio River Valley, discoveries of massive man-made mounds began to be described in their journals and diaries. For the most part, these seemed to be burial grounds, some containing human bones, others the ashes of human bones. Some did not. As well, many contained artifacts completely foreign to their location and out of keeping with the Native American life the settlers observed around them.

The Miamisburg Mound is the largest conical burial mound in the state of Ohio and possibly in the eastern United States. Archaeological investigations of the surrounding area suggest that it was constructed by the prehistoric Adena Indians (800 BC–AD 100). Built on a 100-foot-high bluff, the mound measures 877 feet in circumference. It was originally more than 70 feet high. Visitors to Montgomery County should stop off at Mound Avenue and climb the 116 steps from its base to the summit for a view of the surrounding 37-acre park.

History—Chronology

Giant Classroom Ohio History Timeline

Requirements:
Lots of wall space, oversize butcher paper, markers or chalk, found materials

Time:
30 days

The Project:
Make a three-dimensional Ohio History Timeline

The Pizzazz!
Kids like big! Create educational and emotional impact by creating a gigantic timeline no one could miss!

Here's how:
Think HUMONGOUS! Use every inch of space available to create a 3-foot or wider state history timeline. Make it as long as possible and around all four walls! Start with early peoples, exploration period, colonial period, etc. Write significant dates with large markers. Students can draw in marker, crayon, or colored chalk to create appropriate scenes. Bring the timeline right on around to the present. In fact, you can allow the last wall to be an ongoing timeline, added to as significant Ohio history continues to take place. It's less important that this timeline be neat than it is dramatic. Three-dimensional projects can be taped or glued to the timeline. Don't forget women's history, all of Ohio's minority groups, contemporary war history, and other things, just because they don't appear in your textbooks. Here's your chance to show students just how important history really is!

Tip:
The Rose Center for Earth and Space in New York City adopted this giant timeline concept. They even left slats in the floor that can be moved to add a few million years here and there as new facts about the age of the universe are determined!

Correlates with History A.1

History—Settlement

What is Ohio history, anyway? History is:

- 1. Anything that happened in the past.
- 2. Anything that you are doing today (since it will instantly be Ohio "history"—so think before you act!)
- 3. Anything you might do tomorrow, or next week, month, year, etc.

There are all types of history. Geologic history includes the booms and bangs and grates and grinds that Mother Nature and outer space visitors like meteorites inflict upon our state.

Prehistoric history sounds like it isn't even possible! But it doesn't mean things happened in Ohio before there was history, just before we had writers and reporters and cameras and video to document events. We have to rely on "evidence," such as the fossils of giant Jurassic cockroaches, to know what happened way back when.

History of people is the most perplexing, confusing, and misleading history of all. Why? Probably because people decide what is historically important enough to record for posterity. People decide WHO was important, and so, because they leave other people out, who wasn't important (at least in their opinion!)

PEOPLE HISTORY is very important! There are many reasons for this. Just a few of them include:

- Ohio people make good history, and bad history.
- The history of Ohio people helps tell us who we are.
- We use what people have or have not done in the past in our state to help us decide what to do or not do in the present and the future.

Correlates with History B.2

Famous Ohioans

Here are a few Famous Ohioans who made history!

John Heisman (1869–1936)
Cleveland, Ohio
The Heisman Trophy to recognize the nation's outstanding collegiate football player is named for this early football pioneer.

Toni Morrison (b. 1931)
Lorain, Ohio
Toni Morrison is an African-American author who has received many literary awards, among them the Pulitzer Prize in 1988.

Annie Oakley (1860–1926)
Patterson Township, Darke County, Ohio
Annie Oakley became a legendary sharpshooter while touring the country with Buffalo Bill and his Wild West Show.

William Tecumseh Sherman (1820–1891) Lancaster, Ohio (Farfield County)
Ranked second only to General Ulysses S. Grant as the greatest Northern general during the Civil War.

Ted Turner (b. 1938)
Cincinnati, Ohio
Known as a successful businessman and a cable-television pioneer, Ted Turner turned philanthropist in 1998 when he pledged $1 billion to the United Nations.

Some people, mostly never written about in history books, had to get out there and discover our state! This included all types of people for all kinds of reasons. Perhaps your relative carried a flintlock rifle and trudged through mountain passes to get to our state? Or maybe came to our state in a covered wagon? Worked to build railroads? Panned for gold? Traded furs? Was a lumberjack?

Where would Ohio be today without the everyday people who came to claim it and tame it? Some worked to improve laws and enforce them. Others built churches or did missionary work. Some slogged their way across new landscapes to map the terrain for those who would follow. Others came to report on the wonders of America that most people had not seen yet.

History—Settlement

Fallen Timbers Battlefield

The Fallen Timbers Battlefield is both historical and new. It was the site of a famous and important event in American history. Yet the exact location where the 1794 battle between General Anthony Wayne's army and a confederacy of American Indian tribes took place was discovered more than 200 years later. Preserving the Fallen Timbers Battlefield is important to learn about military and social events that took place in the Maumee Valley that led directly to Ohio becoming a state.

For many years, a monument to the battle has stood on a bluff overlooking the Maumee River. Many thought that the battle took place on the high spot and the floodplain below. But G. Michael Pratt, an anthropologist and faculty member at Heidelberg College, believed that the battle occurred about a quarter-mile away.

In 1995, Pratt conducted the first archaeological survey in a farm field at the northwest corner of the intersection of US 24 and US 23/I-475 in Maumee, Ohio. A significant number of artifacts dating to the late 1700s supported his theory, and subsequent surveys revealed additional evidence that intense fighting took place on the site.

At the same time, a group of citizens called the Fallen Timbers Battlefield Preservation Commission organized to advocate for the battlefield's protection. In 2000, Metroparks of the Toledo area reached an agreement to buy a 187-acre site considered to be a key portion of the battlefield site. The same year, Congress established the Fallen Timbers Battlefield and Fort Miamis National Historic Site and designated it as an Affiliated Unit of the National Park Service.

Metroparks completed buying the property with local, state, and federal funds in the fall of 2001. Immediately, The Fallen Timbers Advisory Commission was formed to plan the future of the historic site.

Correlates with History B.3

The Wright Brothers

How did Orville and Wilbur Wright get the idea to create some kind of craft that would really fly? The seed of this idea was planted in their young minds when their father brought a toy helicopter home from a business trip in the late 1870s.

The two brothers grew up in Dayton, Ohio. As young adults, they built and repaired bicycles for a living. During the slow winter months, the brothers studied one favorite subject: flight. They studied birds, built kites, and analyzed historical information about man's many attempts to fly.

Through their studies, Orville and Wilbur realized that when air moved over a wing that was "warped" (curved at the top), it provided "lift" to the wing. If lift could help get a glider off the ground and keep it in the sky longer, could a pilot control the lift of an aircraft?

The Wright brothers built a glider and headed for Kitty Hawk, North Carolina because of the consistent sea breeze there. Just as they expected, one of them could lay face downward on the glider, catch the offshore breeze, tug at the lines to control the wings, and fly in the air over the sand! Flights were short, lasting five to ten seconds and traveling only 20 to 30 feet across the sand. But it was a start!

Orville and Wilbur went back to Dayton for more experiments. In 1901 and 1902, they returned to Kitty Hawk, setting gliding records with various improvements to their craft. After more study and experimentation, Wilbur and Orville added a gasoline engine and a specially-designed propeller to their glider.

On December 17, 1903, Orville Wright piloted their flying machine on an incredible trip lasting 12 seconds. It was the first time that any machine carrying a person had raised itself by its own power into the air in full flight. What an amazing story of determination by two brothers!

● Talk to students about the qualities in the Wright Brothers that led to their success. It didn't happen overnight—their historic flight took desire, imagination, study, patience, experimentation, and determination!

Correlates with History C.6

Airplanes Everywhere!

It's simply amazing how quickly flight advanced after the Wright brothers' success at Kitty Hawk in 1903. By the time Orville Wright died in 1948, he had lived long enough to see airplanes with enclosed cockpits and passenger cabins, jet engines, and the breaking of the sound barrier. Now we have rocket engines, aircraft flying at supersonic speeds, jet engine helicopters, Harrier jets that take off straight up, and the space shuttle!

In 1953, 29 years after their famous first flight, an enormous granite memorial built atop Kill Devil Hill, North Carolina was dedicated to Orville and Wilbur Wright. Another memorial to the Wright brothers is located in the National Air and Space Museum in Washington, D.C. The original *Flyer* hangs there as a reminder of the history that took place one cold winter's day at Kitty Hawk.

Cultural Comparisons

Read me a story: Read stories from all over the world. Read stories from different parts of the United States. Discuss the different cultures represented. How many differences can the students recognize: food, clothing, art, literature, celebrations, or family structure?

Parlez-vous? How many different languages do your students speak? Is English a second language for any of them?

My roots are showing: Have students research their proud heritages and create a family tree. How far back in time can they go? Have them present their reports to the class. How many different cultures are represented? How are they different? How are they the same? How have various cultures blended to create a multi-cultural society in the United States?

My life... Have students create a poster showing the person who's had the greatest influence on their life. Use drawings, photographs, and maps.

We're all in this together: Discuss social institutions and name several in your community. Identify people who are involved. Find articles and pictures to create a class collage.

People In Societies

From the time we're born, we belong to many different groups. We are humans from Planet Earth. We are members of a gender group. We are members of a race. We inhabit a continent. We are citizens of a country. We are members of a society. We are members of a culture. We are part of a community. We live in a neighborhood. We belong to a family. We have friends. We work. We play. We worship. Wow! If we didn't pay attention, we could really lose track! (How many of these different groups can the students identify? What other groups can the students think of?)

From the moment we're born, we enter into many different relationships. At first, our awareness of these relationships is limited to those whom we can see and touch—our mother and father (or other caregivers), then other family members and friends. As we grow, our awareness increases—as does the number and complexity of our relationships. We have many wants to be satisfied and many needs to be met!

As we can see, no one stands alone! As we go through life, we must understand these numerous groups and relationships. We are connected! In a crowded world that's growing smaller by the day, we must be able to accept, understand, and appreciate our differences.

We must teach our students that we are members of a diverse society—a multi-cultural society. Our society encompasses many distinct cultures. Cultures are not inherent, but are taught to young members. Cultures are reflected in beliefs and values, language, art, customs, institutions, and technology.

Correlates with People in Societies A.1

People In Societies—Cultures

Fort Ancient

Fort Ancient features 18,000 feet of earthen walls built 2,000 years ago by American Indians, who used the shoulder blades of deer, split elk antler, clamshell hoes, and digging sticks to dig the dirt. They then carried the soil in baskets holding 35 to 40 pounds. Portions of these walls were used in conjunction with the sun and moon to provide a calendar system for these people.

When European settlers first entered the Ohio River Valley and the valleys of the Great and Little Miami Rivers, they discovered thousands of earthen mounds and what appeared to them to be earthen fortifications. As the settlers cleared the dense forests, they also plowed under the earthen mounds for farming. It is sad and tragic to contemplate just how many of the Adena and Hopewell earthen structures and mounds have been lost to history. Early settlers did not know that Native Americans had accomplished such engineering feats. The belief arose in a pre-historic non-Indian culture that must have created these earthen structures.

Today, the Museum at Fort Ancient has an education classroom with a number of hands-on areas depicting daily life of American Indians as well as a timeline. There is a prehistoric garden adjacent to the building that offers a look at the agricultural plants and methods of the first Ohioans.

Correlates with People in Societies A.1

The Great Serpent Mound is located in rural Adams County, Ohio, east of Cincinnati. Stretching a quarter mile, Serpent Mound is the largest serpent effigy known to this day. The base of the mound is constructed of rock and clay. The soil that covers the rock is between four and five feet thick. The mound was built on top of a remarkably unique structure that has caused it to become misshapen over the years. Some people say the shape looks like a serpent with its mouth open about to eat an egg, while others say the serpent is about to eat a frog! The serpent extends to the west; because of this, some think that the oval represents the setting sun.

The function of Serpent Mound is somewhat mysterious. It is most likely a religious symbol. Symbolically, the serpent has stood for many things, such as eternity and evil. The Adena could have built the mound as a gift to their god or to ward off any evil.

Amish Dress Codes

Answers to many questions about the Amish, Mennonite, and other "Plain People" can be found at: http://www.800padutch.com

Amish women do not cut their hair and at a very young age begin to wear it up. Women and girls wear a prayer covering most or all of the time. For housework or other chores, they may replace it with a kerchief in order not to mess up their usual prayer covering. Unmarried girls wear a black covering to church starting from the time they are teenagers. Married women generally wear white caps.

Like the women, Amish men wear their hair in simple fashions, most often in a bowl cut. Amish men wear hats most of the time. A hat would never be worn in church and most of the time they would remove their hats before going indoors. Little boys are often seen outdoors without hats more than men are, but boys wear the same type of hat as their fathers. In the summer, most men wear straw hats for working outside. For formal occasions, Amish men wear black felt hats.

The Amish

Approximately one third of all Amish reside in Ohio and there are significant Amish populations in at least 21 Ohio counties. Several of these populations are relatively large and the largest of all Amish settlements is located in the Wayne/Holmes county area.

Most Amish groups do not oppose modern medicine. Their readiness to seek health services varies from family to family. Nothing in the Amish understanding of the Bible forbids them from using modern medical services, including surgery, hospitalization, dental work, anesthesia, blood transfusions, etc. They do believe, however, that good health, both physical and mental, is a gift from God and requires careful stewardship on the part of the individual. With few exceptions, physicians rate the Amish as desirable patients: they are stable, appreciative, and their bills will be paid. They do not have insurance, but they band together to help pay medical expenses for anyone of their group who needs financial assistance.

Old Order Amish forbid photography of their people. Their objection is based on the second commandment, Exodus 20:4: "Thou shalt not make unto thee any graven image, or any likeness of anything that is in heaven above, or that is in the earth beneath, or that is in the water under the earth."

Amish families do play games and read together in the evenings. Parents are involved in their children's activities. However, there are not long evenings in an Amish family. When the children get home from school, there are chores that must be done. At an early age, children have responsibilities assigned to them. After the evening meal, the school homework must be tackled, and before long it is bedtime. Amish are early risers and therefore go to bed early.

Correlates with People in Societies A.1

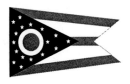

People In Societies—Cultures

Welcome to Ohio

Ohioans have come to the state from other states and many other countries on almost every continent! As time has gone by, Ohio's population has grown more diverse. This means that people of different races and from different cultures and ethnic backgrounds have moved to Ohio.

The French were the first Europeans to see Lake Erie. Do you know who the first person to see the Ohio River was? It was René-Robert Cavelier, Sieur de La Salle, a Frenchman, who may have even gotten as far as Louisville, Kentucky. Do you know when the English arrived in Ohio? In 1685, English fur traders from New York came, and 50 years later people started coming here from the Carolinas, Virginia, and Pennsylvania. Americans and Indians fought over Ohio all through the 1700s.

The first permanent settlement in Ohio was at Marietta in 1788. By 1800, there were 45,000 settlers in Ohio. In 1830, the population of the state was near 1 million, and large numbers of Irish and German immigrants were moving into Ohio. Soon, immigrants from England, France, Wales, and Scotland arrived. The foreign-born population of Ohio in 1880 was 15% of the total population of 3 million. Do you know how many foreign-born people that is? That's 450,000 immigrants who came to Ohio over 50 years!

Ohio's population has grown steadily over the years. Today, there are over 11 million people living in our state. Most are people from German, Italian, Polish, and English ancestry, but there are also many African Americans and a large Hispanic population. Four times as many people live in Ohio's cities than in the country.

Correlates with People in Societies A.1

Geography—Places and Regions

The Effect of Lake Erie!

Landforms can have a tremendous effect on surrounding communities. Ohio and other states along the Great Lakes are home to an interesting weather phenomenon known as "lake-effect snow." These snow events usually occur in late autumn and winter before the lake surface cools to around 32° F or freezes in late winter.

From November 9-14, 1996, the Cleveland area was hit with one of the worst lake-effect snowstorms in the Great Lakes region over the past 50 years. More than 160,000 people lost power, and isolated snowfall amounts came close to 70 inches!

What causes lake-effect snow (LES)? In the winter, cold air from Canada flows over warmer Great Lakes water. Great amounts of heat and water vapor are drawn into these air masses. Clouds form, and the water in the clouds falls back to the ground as snow. LES events usually occur from November to February.

LES showers fall in bands, blanketing one area with snow while another location just a few miles away receives only flurries! Plus, lake-effect snow can fall with a furious intensity. Many of the heaviest snowfalls in the country have resulted from lake-effect snow. Buffalo, New York is probably the most famous recipient of this winter wonder. In December 1995, the city was crippled by 38 inches of snow in just 24 hours!

The primary snowbelt in northeast Ohio includes the extreme northeast corner of the state. This includes Lake, Geauga, Ashtabula, and the eastern part of Cuyahoga counties. Another snowbelt runs through communities south of Cleveland, including Summit, Medina, Portage, and Trumbull counties. The combination of high elevation and the right wind direction can bring heavy LES events to these areas.

Correlates with Geography B.5

Geography

Ohio "Jography": A Fun Run Around the State

A fun way to study geography is to start with an Ohio map. Give each student a road map of Ohio. Then test map-reading skills by asking questions regarding cardinal directions, relative location, etc. (Which body of water forms Ohio's southern border? Northern border? Which state borders Ohio to the East? West? North? South?)

Ask kids to write down all the names of towns they have visited. Write down names of towns they have lived. Write down names of towns they would like to visit and why. Write down names of towns that sound unique. Write down names of towns that students know were named for another place (i.e. Delaware County, Bath township, villages of Lima, Versailles, Zoar, etc.)

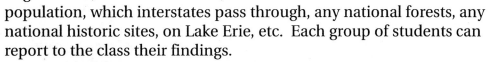

Divide students into groups and assign each group a quarter of the state. Then ask each group of students to identify each quarter's largest cities, natural resources, population, which interstates pass through, any national forests, any national historic sites, on Lake Erie, etc. Each group of students can report to the class their findings.

Are We There Yet?

Use a map with a scale to teach students how far it is from one place to another. Students could use a ruler, another straightedge, or even a piece of paper to figure out distances from one place to another on a map. If students are using a piece of paper, they can put it next to the scale on a map and then mark on the paper the distance equivalent.

Correlates with Geography A.1-3

Geography—Places and Regions

Birdseed Mining Activity

This activity will illustrate how the process of mining works. Students will be able to experience the difficulty that miners face in locating valuable mineral deposits. They will also learn a simple lesson in economics — a less valuable commodity may be more profitable because it is more abundant. Students will be shown the importance of clean, environmentally conscious mining, and will learn that all mining operations must pay for reclamation work.

1. Divide students into groups of 4 to 6.
2. Pour approximately 1 pound of birdseed in each pan.
3. Add 2 gold beads, 4 silver beads and 8 blue beads, and 3 white beads to each pan – mix into birdseed.
4. The beads and seeds represent the following:
   • Gold beads = Gold   • Silver beads = Silver
   • Blue beads = Coal   • Sunflower seeds = Copper
   • All other seeds = Waste
   • White beads = Reclamation   (These beads will be assigned a COST rather than a VALUE because reclamation must be done at all mining operations regardless of how much profit was made.)
5. Students search through the seed mixture and "mine" beads, sunflower seeds, and other grain products, making piles of each. Allow 5 to 10 minutes for the mining activity. (NOTE: The instructor should hint to the students that they should mine NEATLY, not mixing waste seeds with their beads, sunflower seeds and not scattering seeds all over the area. Instructor can have the option of examining the work of each group, or assigning a helper to monitor each group to see how cleanly the "mining" is being done.
6. Assign a value for each type of bead or seed.
7. Have the students count up the number of gold, silver, and blue beads, and sunflower seeds from their piles and multiply the number of each by their values given in #6. Document all information on a separate sheet of paper. Students should also note the amount of any environmental damage fines on the spreadsheet. Students should count the number of white beads in their pile and multiply by the reclamation factor. This number should be recorded on each group's paper.
8. Have each group total up the dollar value of their "mining" operation, subtracting the environmental damage fines and reclamation costs. Have each group share their success with the others. Prizes may be awarded to the best table of "miners."

Correlates with Geography B.6

Geography—Human Environmental Interaction

Lake Erie—Making a Comeback!

By the end of the 1960s, Lake Erie was dying. The quality of the water was so bad that all swimming was forbidden. The natural plant and animal life of the lake was disappearing fast. The busy transportation throughout the lake was killing it. Wastes from factories, cities, and farms had been polluting the lake for over a hundred years. Poisons such as mercury were killing the lake's wildlife.

In the 1970s Canada and the United States joined forces to clean up Lake Erie. Measures were taken to keep dangerous substances from entering the waters. Poisonous levels of mercury have decreased and species of fish that had almost disappeared returned. It seems that Lake Erie has been restored to life!

Eutrophication

Eutrophication is the aging of a lake by biological enrichment of its water. In a young lake the water is cold and clear, supporting little life. With time, streams draining into the lake introduce nutrients such as nitrogen and phosphorus, which encourage the growth of aquatic organisms. As the lake's fertility increases, plant and animal life burgeons, and organic remains begin to be deposited on the lake bottom. Over the centuries, as silt and organic debris pile up, the lake grows shallower and warmer, with warm-water organisms supplanting those that thrive in a cold environment. Marsh plants take root in the shallows and begin to fill in the original lake basin. Eventually the lake gives way to bog, finally disappearing into land. Depending on climate, size of the lake, and other factors, the natural aging of a lake may span thousands of years.

Pollutants can radically accelerate the aging process. During the past century, lakes in many parts of the earth have been severely eutrophied by pollution. Many pollutants act as plant nutrients. They stimulate the growth of algae, create unsightly green scum and smelly odors, and rob the water of dissolved oxygen vital to other aquatic life. At the same time, other pollutants flowing into a lake may poison whole populations of fish; whose decomposing remains further deplete the water's dissolved oxygen content. This can literally choke a lake to death.

Correlates with Geography C.9

Economics

Kids are consumers. They are often consumed with the problem of wants versus needs (who isn't?)! Making economic choices, especially first saving and then spending, are important skills for young people to learn. They're never too young to begin to learn about cash versus credit, taxes, banking, economic interdependence, and almost everything else associated with economics.

All too often young people are hired on at a company, and like most businesses, the company is disappointed to realize that their new employee did not even understand the simple vocabulary of business—invoice, asset, liability, withholding, etc. Most educators will agree that this lack of knowledge puts young people at an immediate disadvantage in the workplace.

But now that you're teaching economics, your students will leave your classroom with the bonus of knowing more about money and how it works at school, at home, at work, in the state, the nation, and around the world! This will be a real "asset" to them! They'll be able to make informed consumer choices and use resources more effectively. This knowledge helps each individual and our society, too!

Tell students that money has a role in all societies. Even if it is not money as they know it today. Even if it is shells strung on a thread and called wampum. Even if it is barter where corn equals money.

Money is convenient. We can spread it out and look at it; stack it up and count it. But as money becomes more "invisible," handled electronically and over the Internet, then it becomes even more important for kids to understand money's role as a medium of exchange.

Correlates with Economics C.5

Economics—Scarcity and Resource Allocation

★ **Economics for Kids** ★

Why that's a capital idea!

It was easy for the Native Americans to look at guns and decide that a heaping pile of tobacco, other crops, or furs, was worth giving away to get these new powerful weapons. Today, it is trickier for a child to see whether their hard-earned allowance is better spent on trading cards now, or saved for college tuition to be paid far in the future.

Americans enjoy a "free enterprise" form of economy that's ruled by the laws of supply and demand. This doesn't mean things are free—it means that people are free to do as they please as far as what they buy and sell (legally, of course!). Except for some licensing fees, and some necessary regulations, people can "manage their [economic] house" the way they see fit without stringent governmental interference.

How do Ohioans make their living? Ohio produces a wide variety of goods and is one of the nation's leading manufacturing states. Fifty-three of the nation's five hundred largest corporations have their headquarters in Ohio. Among them are such giants as Procter & Gamble Company, in Cincinnati; Goodyear Tire & Rubber Company, in Akron; National Cash Register Company, in Dayton; Firestone Tire & Rubber Company in Akron; Sherwin-Williams Company, in Cleveland; and Champion Sparkplug Company, in Toledo.

A diverse economy—agricultural, industrial, high-tech, and service industries—has helped Ohio survive economic hard times, such as recession and depression, and remain financially stable.

Correlates with Economics A.2

Off to market! What effects do students think that competition has on the U.S. market economy? Businesses that provide similar products and services compete with one another for customers. Competition causes producers to keep their prices reasonable and quality high.

Does anyone have any questions? Ask adults to come and explain to the class what they do for a living. How did they prepare themselves for their jobs? How did they gain the necessary skills? Include a local entrepreneur. If adults are not available, students can conduct interviews and report their data to the class.

My projection is…. Make a graph or chart to project sales over the next 10 years. Select a product, choose prices now— higher and lower. Graph or chart the projected supply. Now use the same product. Again, choose prices in 10 years—higher or lower. Graph or chart the projected demand.

Your total is…. Have the class bring in various sales receipts. Calculate the sales tax. Discuss how the government might use this tax money.

Citizenship—Participation

Who Can Become President?
The U.S. Constitution lists three qualifications to be president. The candidate must be a natural born citizen of the United States, must be at least 35 years old, and must have lived in the United States for at least 14 years.

Who Can Vote?
Voting requirements in Ohio include:
● Must be a citizen of the United States
● Must be a resident of Ohio
● Must be 18 years old on or before election day
● Must not be convicted of a felony or currently incarcerated
● Must not be found incompetent by a court for purposes of voting

What About Other States?
Each state has similar rules regarding voter registration, but they are not exactly the same. The state of North Dakota is unusual—it does not require voter registration at all! The state abolished voter registration in 1951.

Understanding Political Parties

When students study the voting process, questions are bound to come up regarding political parties. What are they? What's a Republican? What's a Democrat? What's an Independent? What's the difference?

The main way we elect people to public office in the United States is through political parties. Explain that a political party is a group of people who think alike about how to govern the nation. People choose a party that matches their own beliefs and ideas.

Political parties want to get members elected to federal, state, and local offices so that their ideas will spread everywhere. Staff members in offices around the country help organize campaign events and fundraisers to help their candidates win elections. Some students' parents may have been involved in a political campaign or two.

Voters can also vote as an "independent," which means they don't belong to any particular political party, but just vote for the person they think will do the best job, no matter their party affiliation. In today's world, where people have access to a lot of information about candidates, independent voting is more common than it was in previous generations.

● To bring the concept of political parties closer to home, have students take a look at the elected officials in their state and local area. Is the governor of Ohio a Republican or a Democrat? Is the mayor in their town a Republican or Democrat? What are the party affiliations of their senators and congressmen?

● Show students the symbols of the Democratic party (donkey) and the Republican party (elephant). Both of them originated in political cartoons in the 19th century.

Correlates with Citizenship Rights and Responsibilities A.1a

Government

We the people... of the United States

Freedom! Powerful principles! Fair rules and just laws! Democratic government! Today, we can truly understand how important these ideals are to us in the modern world.

They were pretty important to our founding fathers, too! Which is why they fought so valiantly for independence! I'm sure your students can imagine why the colonists became disenchanted with being "bossed around" by a distant "parent," when they were the ones fighting the Native Americans, felling the trees, planting the crops, building the towns, suffering from the heat, cold, disease, and really big mosquitoes!

We need only to look at the nightly news from around the world to get a glimpse of life without a democratic government and civics (the study of civic affairs and the rights and duties of citizens). Life without civics is life without law. There can be no civics without citizens. But being a citizen is not enough! You have to be a responsible citizen! An informed citizen! A citizen who cares! A citizen who acts! This is not always as easy as it sounds. In some nations, it's difficult to act as a responsible citizen.

No one, not even a school student, should take a good civic life for granted. No one forces good citizenship on people. Good citizenship is not something that comes wrapped like a gift! It's a lot like an education. We say we "get" an education; but no one gives it to us—it is something we achieve ourselves! Good citizenship is the same—you have to create it, protect it, and practice it!

Correlates with Government B.3

Government—Rules and Laws

Bring Ohio Government to Life for Students

Some students might say that a person needs to have lots of money to be elected to office. In these days of television, that's true. If your face and name become familiar to voters, chances are they'll vote for you over someone who can't afford to buy television time. Politicians who have been in office before have the ability to raise money for re-election, which puts them at an advantage over new candidates. Unfortunately, it may also put incumbents at the mercy of those who make large donations to their campaign.

Students may perceive "government" as being something vague, faraway, and not applicable to their daily lives. Cure this by writing the following examples on index cards: Traffic Lights; Clean Water; Trash Pickup; Schools, etc. Put one card face down on each student's desk. Announce: "Sorry, we have NO state or local government today." Go around the room and have each student turn over his or her card and read what it says. To each, respond, "Sorry, there are NO traffic lights," etc. Continue until all the cards have been picked up. Ask students to tell you what government provides them. Ask them if they are glad this activity was just for "pretend"!

Invite a government figure to class. Have them dress casual, if possible, and bring pictures of their family, their favorite golf club, etc., so students can see that they are not just "suits" but Dads, Moms, etc.

Have students ask their parents whether they voted in the last election. If they didn't, ask students to find out why. Voter apathy is a big problem in the United States today. Now is your chance to be a role model and to get your students involved in their government. Some questions to help them (and you!) make a choice in an election:

• Which candidate would you enjoy working with?
• Which candidate has a better work ethic?
• Which candidate would you feel more comfortable introducing to your parents?
• Does the candidate appear intelligent?
• Is he or she qualified by education and experience for the job?
• Is there anything in the candidate's background that concerns you?
• Do you trust the candidate?

Correlates with Government B.4

Citizenship Rights and Responsibilities

★ · ★ ★ ★ ★ ★ ★

A good civic life may seem like our "right" as United States citizens, but it is really a hard-fought and hard-won privilege given to those who practice it and perpetuate it!

To preserve and perpetuate a free society within a democracy, we must have informed and concerned citizens. We have to teach our children how to be responsible citizens who care about their country, their government, their fellow citizens. We must give them opportunities to practice and demonstrate these skills. We must help them realize the value of what we as Americans have and what could be lost. By so doing, we will be preparing them to function successfully as citizens of a global society.

We must teach them for their future—and for ours! To continue to live in a powerful and prosperous country—a productive and cooperative nation, we have to teach our students to recognize potential problems from a country that's becoming increasingly diverse.

On a global level, we must prepare and educate our students so that they, as adults, can recognize potential problems that might be created from a diverse world that's growing smaller and smaller and becoming more interdependent. We must give them the tools now so that they will be able to understand and solve these problems before they arise!

Culture clashes! Disease! Hunger! Overpopulation! War! We must prepare our children so that we can all look forward to a future free of turmoil. To a future of cooperation, peace, and abundance!

Correlates with Citizenship Rights and Responsibilities A.2

The Constitution

The Constitution of the United States of America establishes and protects the citizen's fundamental rights and liberties. The First Amendment covers many different rights:

- Religion: Government may not establish an official religion, nor endorse, or unduly interfere with the free exercise of religion.
- Speech: Individuals are free to express their opinions and beliefs.
- Press: The press has the right to gather and publish information, including that which criticizes the government.
- Assembly: Individuals may peacefully gather.
- Petition: Individuals have the right to make their views known to public officials.

In 1921, Congress made laws restricting immigration. In 1965, Congress passed new legislation that made it easier for immigrants to enter the United States of America.

Immigration and naturalization particularly in the twentieth century have led to an increasingly diverse society. To become a citizen through naturalization, a person must demonstrate knowledge of American history and principles and the ability to speak and write English.

Citizenship—The Rights, Duties, and Responsibilities

A citizen is an individual with certain rights and duties under a government and who, by birth or by choice, owes allegiance to that government. There are two means of obtaining citizenship in the United States:

- Birth
- Naturalization

Do We Have Any Volunteers?

One of the basic responsibilities of citizenship is to contribute to the common good. There are many ways individuals demonstrate responsible citizenship. However, civic responsibilities are fulfilled by choice; they are voluntary.

Responsibilities of Citizens:

- Register and vote
- Hold elective office
- Influence government by communicating with government officials
- Serve in voluntary, appointed positions
- Participate in political campaigns
- Keep informed regarding current issues
- Respect others' rights to an equal voice in government

Correlates with Citizenship Rights and Responsibilities A.1

~ This book is not reproducible. ~

Citizenship Rights and Responsibilities

Few rights, if any, are considered absolute. For example, the guarantee of freedom of religion doesn't mean that the government must allow all religious practices. In the 1800s, some Mormons believed it was a man's religious duty to have more than one wife. The Supreme Court ruled that Mormons had to obey laws forbidding that practice.

Amendment 1: Freedom of religion, speech, and the press; rights of assembly and petition

Congress shall make no law respecting an establishment of religion, or prohibiting the free exercise thereof; or abridging the freedom of speech, or of the press; or the right of the people peaceably to assemble, and to petition the government for a redress of grievances.

Amendment 14: Civil rights

Section 1. All persons born or naturalized in the United States, and subject to the jurisdiction thereof, are citizens of the United States and of the state wherein they reside. No state shall make or enforce any law which shall abridge the privileges or immunities of citizens of the United States; nor shall any state deprive any person of life, liberty, or property, without due process of law; nor deny to any person within its jurisdiction the equal protection of the laws.

The Fourteenth Amendment declares that no state can "deprive any person of life, liberty, or property without due process of law." The Supreme Court has interpreted these words to mean that most of the Bill of Rights applies to the states as well.

Correlates with Citizenship Rights and Responsibilities B.4

A witness is ordered to appear in court by a subpoena. A person who fails to appear in court can be punished for contempt of court. A witness who lies in court is guilty of the crime of perjury, and can be severely punished. Witnesses may legally refuse to testify against themselves or their spouses.

Some people do not volunteer to fulfill their civic responsibilities. That is their choice; but many people see this as a problem. Many people believe that the government is better off if more people are involved. Remember: a basic responsibility of citizenship is to contribute to the common good. The United States government is set up so that citizens can take part in it.

Index